Space Sniper

Prince Sword

Blade Warrior

Celtic Warrior

Super Mom

Jungle Man

Robin Hood

Dragon Queen

Sir-Lance-A-Lot

Hannibal

Super Egor

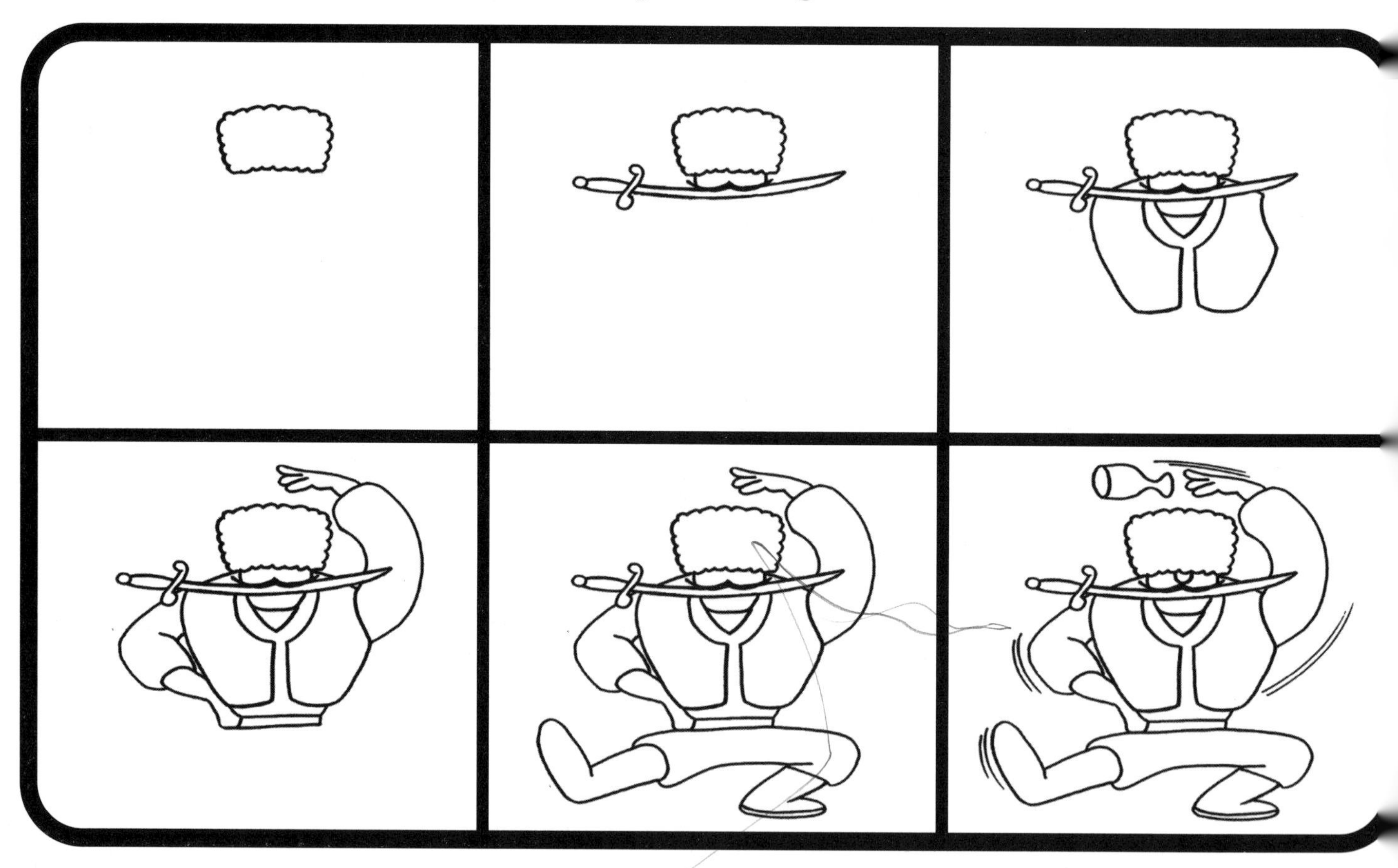

Skater

Super Moose

Volgan

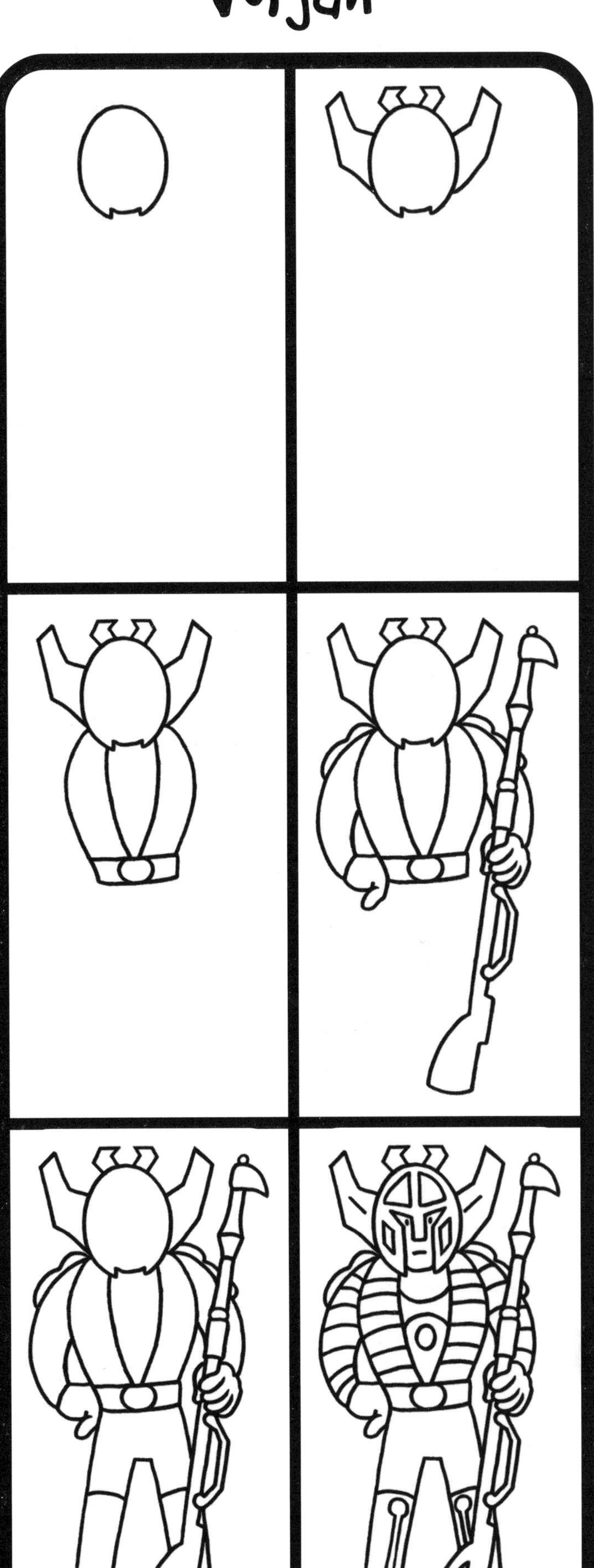

Buffalo Bill

Galactica

Super oil

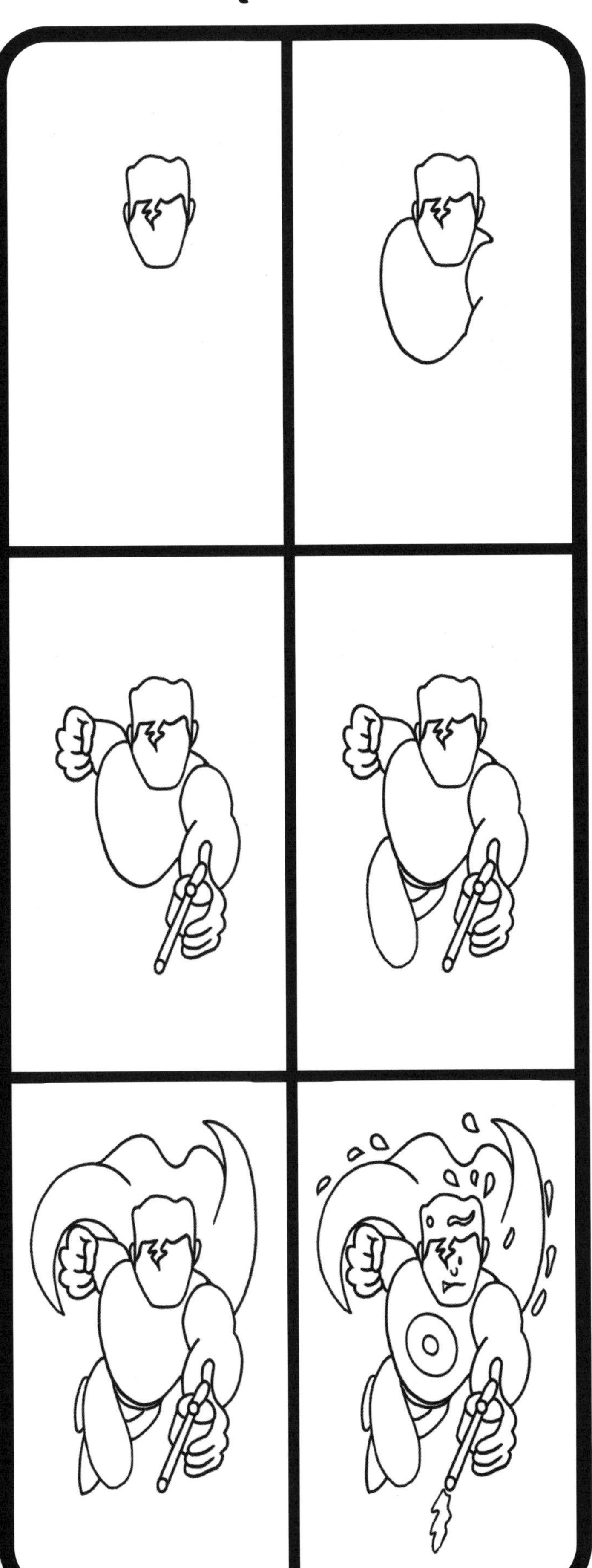

Rope Breaker

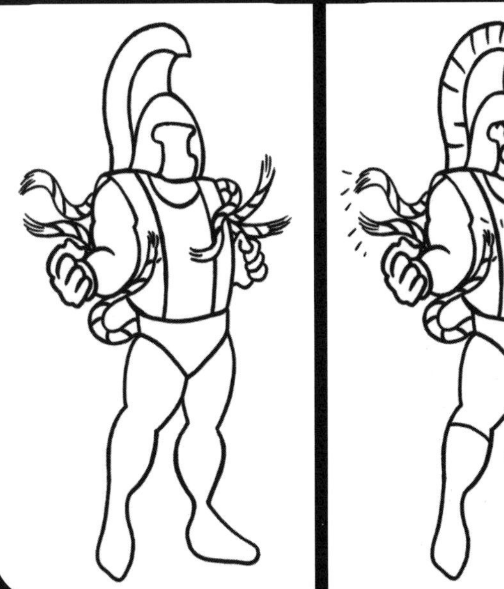

The Bat

Globe Man

Space Robot

Space Baroness

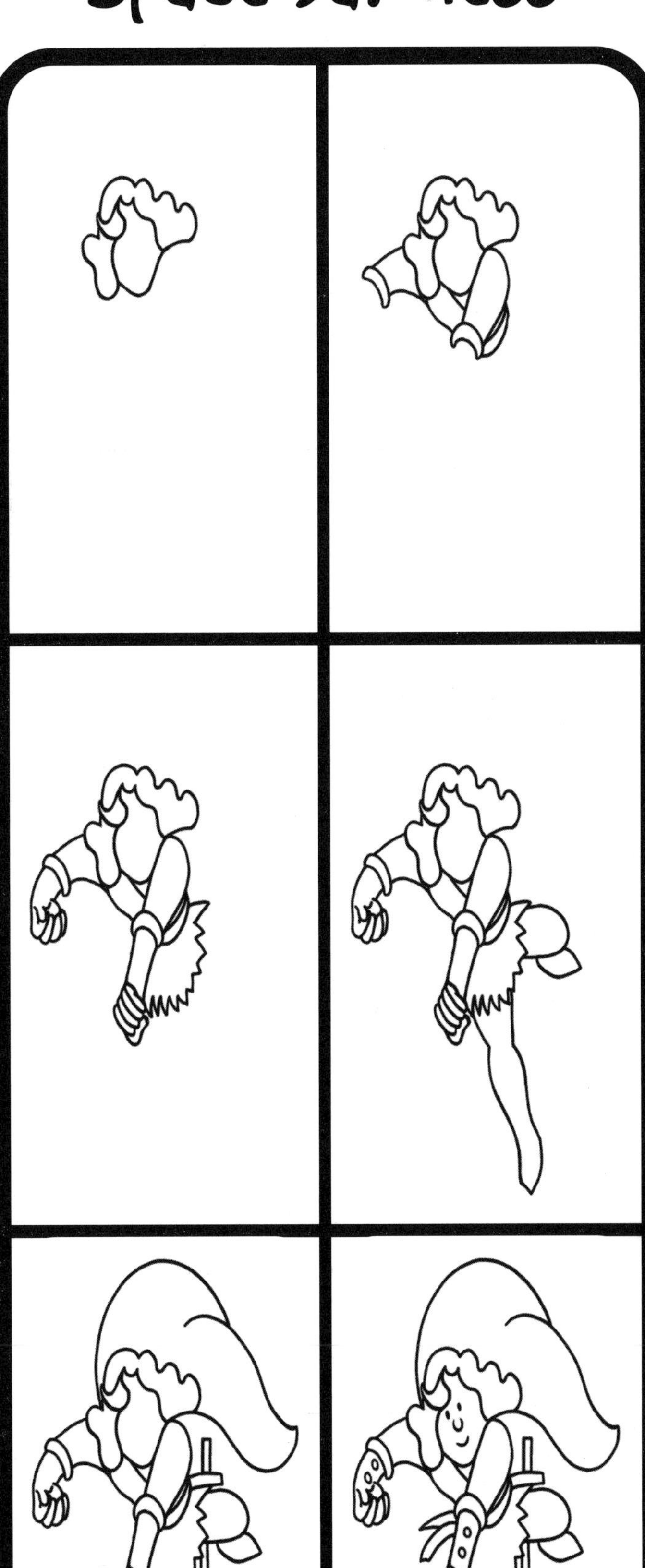

Space Warrior

Sonic Hero

Mechanic Man

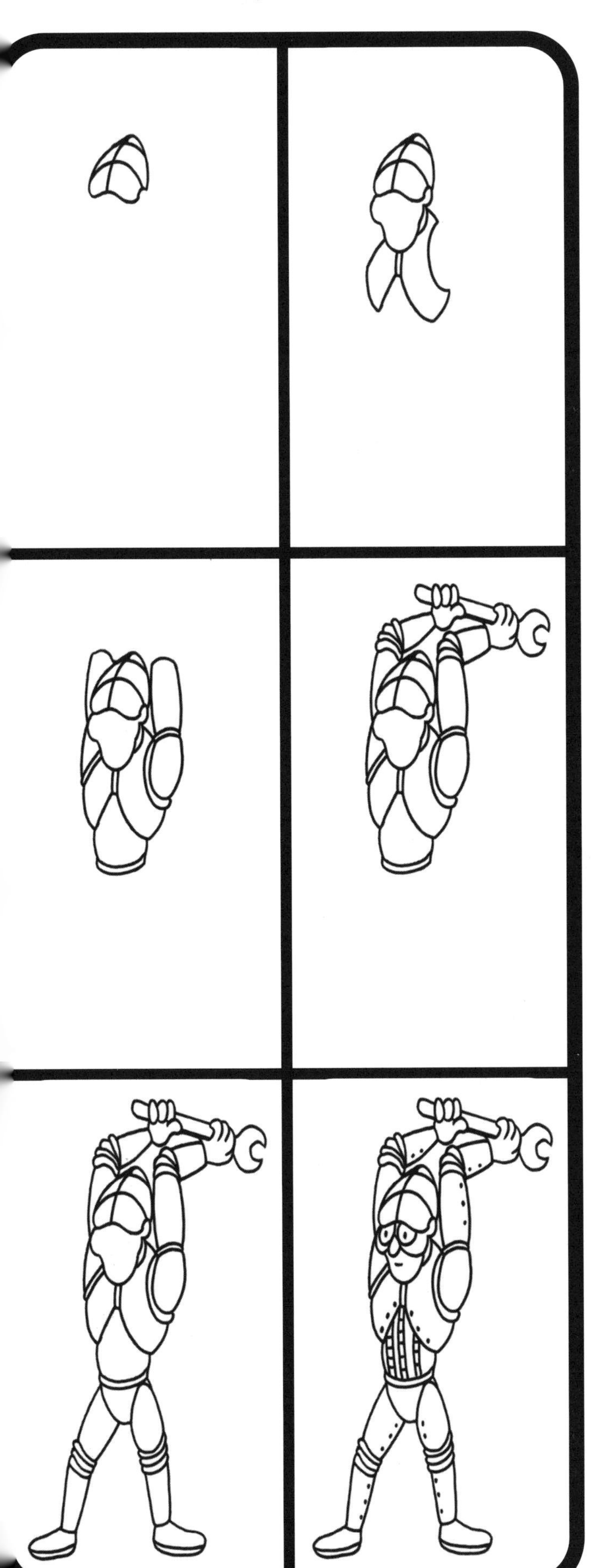

Demon Fighter

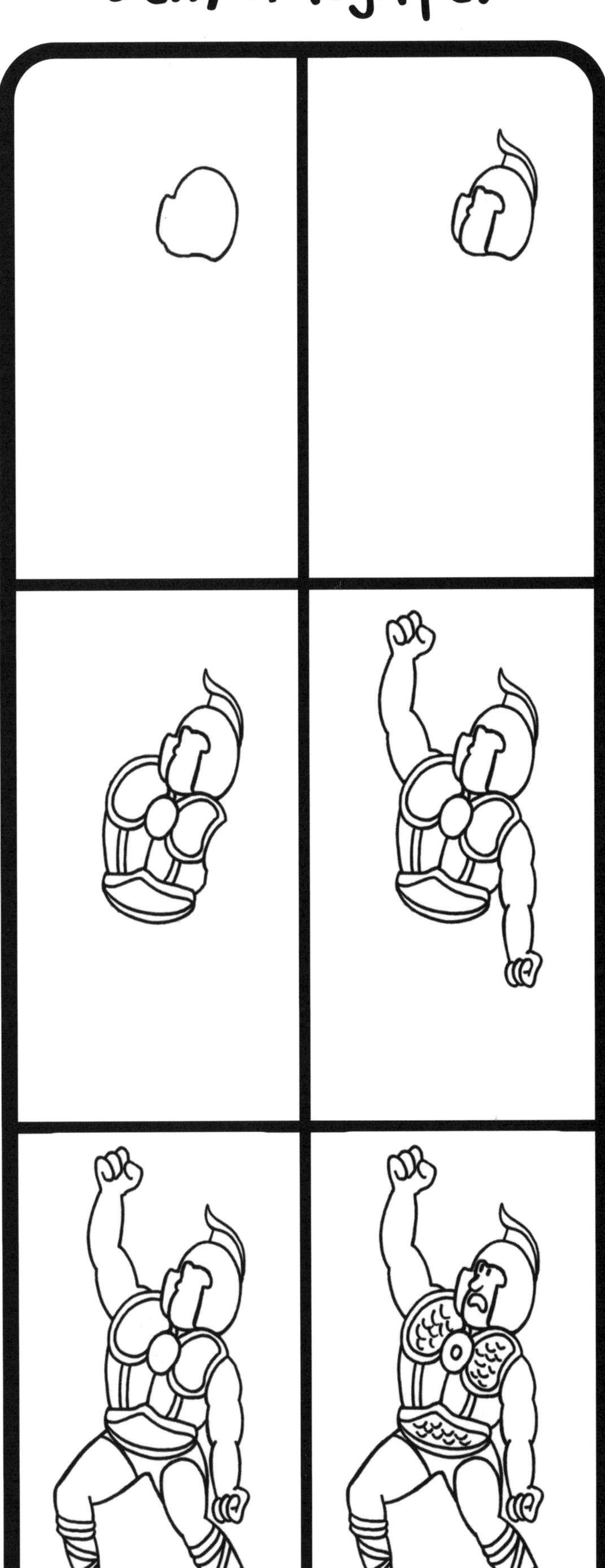

Demon Slayer

Lightning Diver

UDDz

Captain Galactic

Ninja

Axeman

The Archer

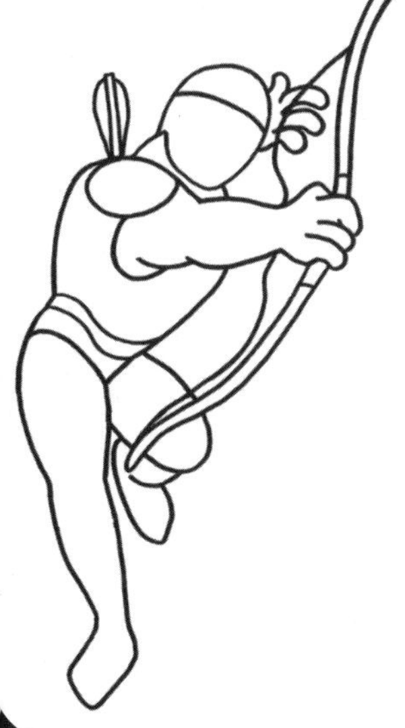

Lightning

Sky Boxer

Venus Amazon

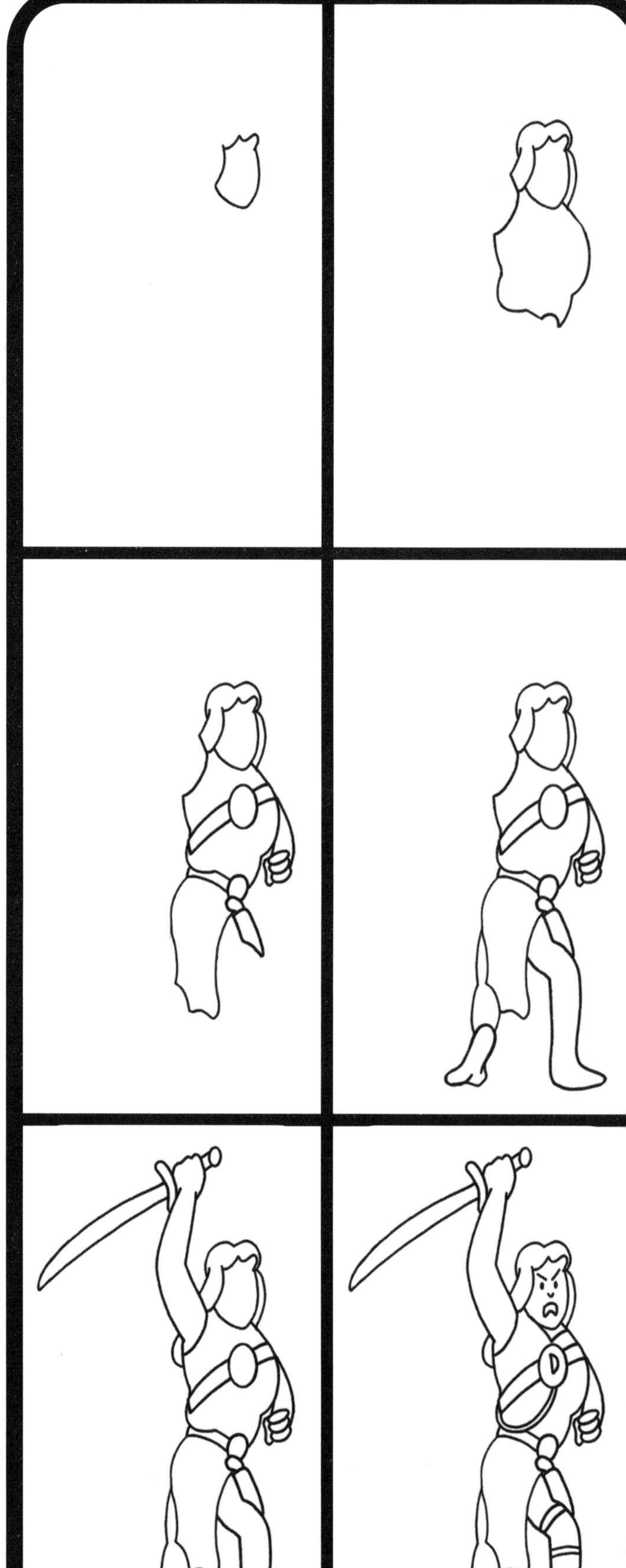

Star Warden

Spartacus

Star Hunter

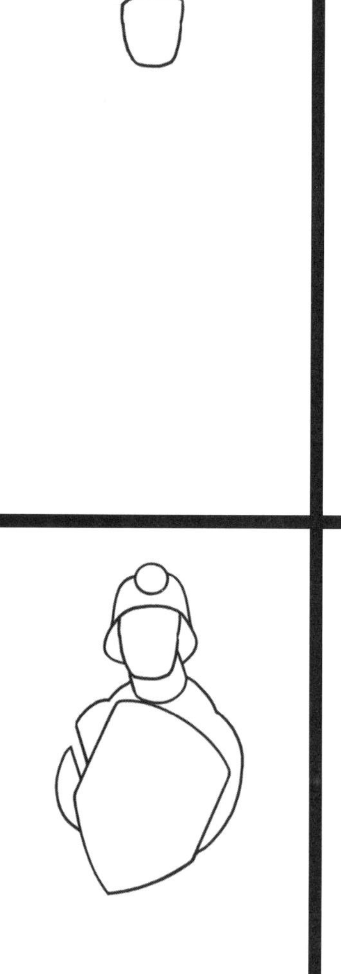

Space Shield

Kajo

Zulu

Queen Boudicca

Aztec

Super Saver

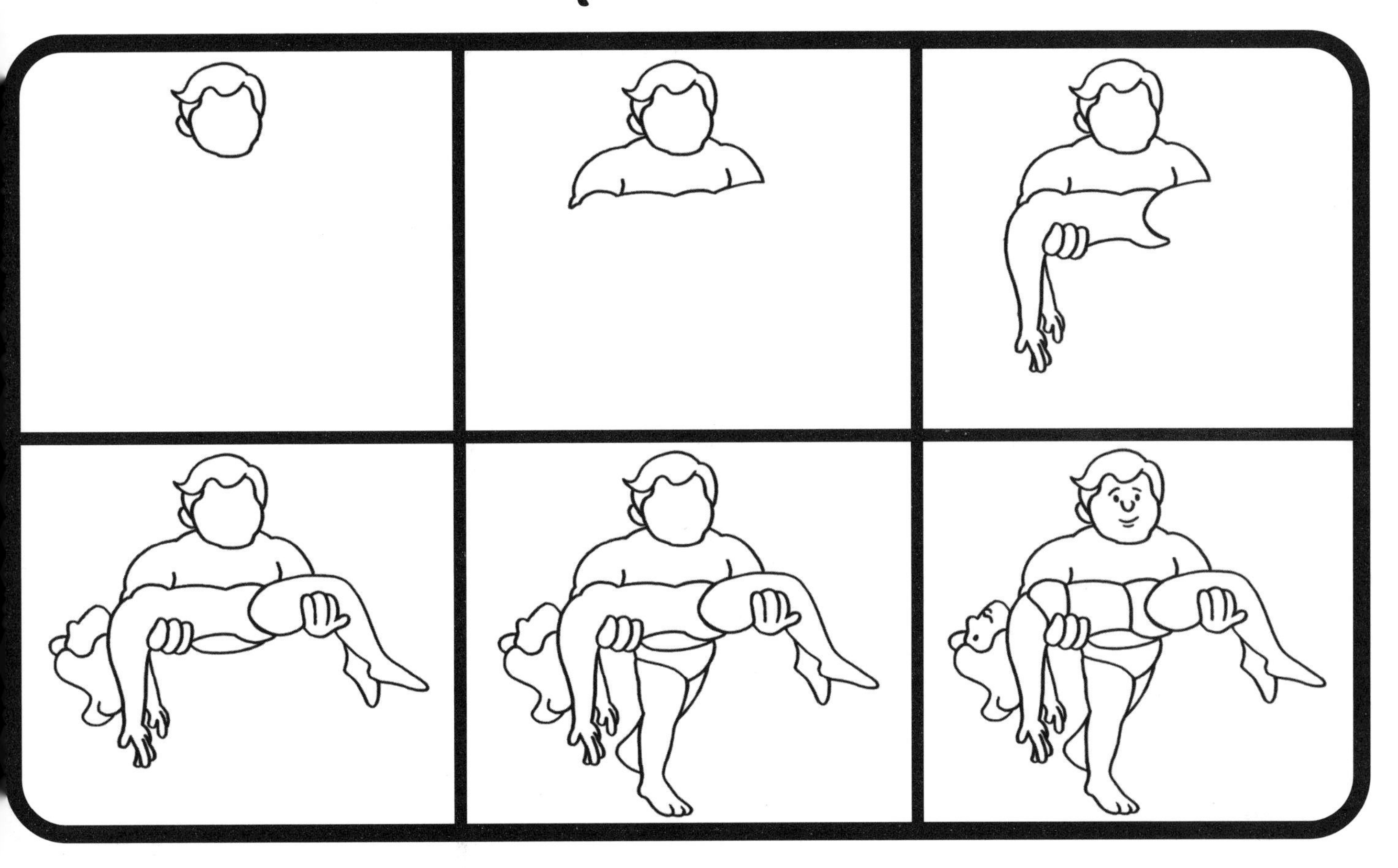

Samurai

Swash Buccaneer

Space Skater